Elliotté P. Joel

Seek the upside eyes, there are two.

To Lucia Slatkovská

“Close the door gently.”
Poetry of Elliotté P. Joel

Old beach

South sound recalls how blind air relishes on young bones. Observation of screaming eyes cradle on crowns of dead fish, treewool dancers disregard past earthly occurrences that life is braided by uneven hand when you can just set the hair free.

Look, the smoke is rising up from dead shoulders. Sweaty women, seraphine, they were the frozen sea, calling, stolen withless pulling the horns of childhood by rotten teeth. We just wanted to live somehow although it came from the lack of love.

Some pig sold him strychnine. Pigs… are better with salt. The beach is better alive. It's so very easy to get attached and walk the plank way bricked by pigeon and chicken feathers to the cottage of calm dull kitchens. Feet. Knees. Stomach. Heart. Head. Crown. Wake up. Get up, it's the unraveled tule of Sunday's white.

How to kill Goethe
Do not let your brunette locks freeze. I will cover you in a still white
coat of acryl paint, I will pay for the olives and walk you home.
The leering distance of my soul is haunting the pleasurehouse – this
is exactly what happens when you look your reflection in the eye.
"Have you ever seen this man?"
I have. Who hasn't? We used to know why am I doing this but
I forgot.
I forgot the olive yards. The yards I have forgotten
levitate somewhere in the sudden aggression of summer storm.
"Once more. You just need to walk this road one last time and you
will be set free."
No longer do I recall words or acts:
I just dreamt that salvation for me has come and then I fell through
the floor into hell.
He cannot reach me through time. "No, I have not seen this man."
I am my own person now.
His harrowing back no longer bents above me for shelter like the
calculus of drearily tender parts of brain...
See me caress through flames:
I am the hell itself.

Somersault
We'd done a lot
to flee their mistreatment.
Should I reinvent
the hollow caged bird?
Somersaults in the gym
scraped the skin
and rubber.
Loose pipes play like church's bells.

The morrowhail of August 1961
Firecrackers in houses, fields, brooks.
It urges us to wear the curtains like an ethereal gown for goddess.
We had a math teacher named Katherine Dee. Everyone was very
mean to her.
Fleshy calves of rooves and drowsing pixie Anemone, and the rain.
The iron thaw slaughtering midday-planted tomatoes in yogurt pots
like an imaginary friend who doesn't love you.
You never know when to stop drinking.
Deluded, delusional fever...
Forget; the aridity of my hurdle to sustain might be the spell of this
city.
Morrowhail keeps infecting the wounded brawls of trying dawn
stained by time
and evening shadows; yours I was, am today and will tomorrow.

Muse of the radio

to E. S.

Heavy are heavens, generous are hours of nothing for the road home is not so long from the integrity of stars. Disordered teacups fathom their beaten saucers in a proud goose lie: your fast train had only two wagons.

Am I thinking about what I am to see? Yet I know exactly, poor ascesis, rope entwoeing you through legs and madhouse pursuit, I am to meet my very own tuberculosis Marína. My very own drunken Adela Ostrolúcka. I see eldrichly little whereas my heart beats slowly always as if closing to death caused by inadequately large knowledge that there is not much difference between dreams and lucidity of days, yet the peacefulness that all thoughts are forgotten when we'll sleep in dirt or when we'll just sleep. Everyone with empathy and somewhat of talent can express a true form of sorrow, yet what geniality does it take to profoundly awaken read joy? Must the two, blackness and the sun within, be coexistent, the hope must live through times of sadness, the misery must caress the light body of brightness.

Hippies on heroin, leather academic approval and starvation on royalties, sleeping oily in deserts – still I am writing poems to you. I had to travel to the hometown to visit a doctor, even drunk from the last night I vomited on a carriage entering. The doc said I cannot drink anymore. It might be my true death, true this time, he said. I am replacing it with a lot of coffee and I usually eat twice a day, nonetheless it had been an experience almost orgasmic, almost martyring, to sense my cells dying, dissolving my consciousness, you know, too, Erik.

As eternally sun's lips awaken, moving as if something that can laugh, that has skin and bones like us, feeling your scent under its nails.

Ruins

Ruminated roominghouse along sheared skins, shaved with intents of spanks for feeding pupils relenting the snow dust. I notice people sweeping their cottages, allocating their thresholds in irregular dust circles, full of spreading earhthaggard balls and men playing cello, praying for vodka. I notice people, I know I'll go to heaven when I die.

This boy in the front cannot cage his sight of me, he is mealing them on my revealed tan and my yolks with whites. Funny how he doesn't know what am I. How I forever plea: "Do not shut the blinds. I want to look at the trees."

Some new observations

There are warts on my right forearm although I cut them out last winter, and the kites are in the sky although they were merciless this autumn. They would brush the lakes with their body hair in five-hour rations until blue bows of girls fled lost in triangles that dark forests weren't able to translate.

No. I am not good at this game. You reply: "Don't worry. It's nothing serious, we'll teach you. Please, at least try. It's even less serious than coffee or racehorses." Then you are angry when I suck at it. I am not playing games ever again, with you nor with anyone else!

Rain attacks wildflower innocence and vigorous wolves howl locked in strawberry sewers. Cigarettes never tasted good except for the beauty of preschool children riding bikes from sidewalk to sidewalk and elderly couples eating ice cream in a tranquil slow movement, dusk-swallowed, on riviera, and weed-weaved hair of virgins with a healthy smile of soon redfoliage, return of eternal self.

Cemetery strawberries, November strawberries. what's the time, dry showing branches, heavy red apples withering on the highest ones? Cholera, dryness of sparrows, they are not seen. I don't remember that story, I remember a rusty pot tossed in thorns and a flash of teeth, the color of sky, woods below and the touched tone of your cold hand carrying an umbrella whilst it didn't rain. You're like a meadow. Grass. Dew. Cow. Sublime wines paying dearly for Jesus' years, stripped, milked, enticing and exfoliated in various hues of death shook in alone naughtly roams and cries for East: Death, my death, this August sprinkling water is a part of every American household.

Ancient beasts

The curl in the window stands there mellow, perceiving a small-town burlesque of reconciling hunger. The even was of more gaiety than all the medallions of his tender hands as he looks for me only in my mind like a dream car in the sea.

Is it wrong to describe pictures drawn in the encyclopedia of Chimeras? Attempting to rhyme on my rubber legs about the embodiment of someone or something that has existed during the long age for not so long and seeking it everywhere like a treasuredeemed imagination... soul shining in a dead spark and time in a beige tint.

Oh, you, standing upon doors that never open in a black coat wooden grace and ginger ballet. The neighbors are complaining because your thoughts are too loud for them. And hazels flowered that each one of us has million eyes: the muse was asleep in the deepest realization of vomit. I shook its shoulder to show her as you vanished through the keyhole.

Bury me under a question mark where the muses are never loved. We just juice them for art of their body and of their soul.

Who'd read poetry in an industrial city?

to You

This might be the thing that will kill you.

But what hasn't been? What has, yet, killed me? Everything just happens to wound, moreover when I witness my death I may still speak by the memory of red plants climbing station gates. I had so many loves that I anymore cannot persevere love in its true kind. Who would even love in this industrial city? There are no sonnets. Only skulls.

There have been many wars. In a blanket of mold I survived everything.

And you are alive, your locks mirror rhythm of pulse. You keep tying them up for in a deep sleep everyone lingers. Brief hellos drink surprise of warm barbiturate songs, there is nothing other to be freed than violent murders of thinking.

Innocence has stanched you by accident's piercing flight, lumbering, seeking why your windows hide before the crime of the deep tarns which had to fashion before my weary eyes.

Should I have reveried of white carnation flower brawls – carnations live very shortly.

A single red rose in a trashcan
Restricted wind
killed the fly
on a lid
of my eye.
The insect flew over my sight
as I opened for the satin light
of my newly born existence.

Your father's guitar
By square walks of a masked night
a ghost was known of me.
It stepped beneath sunflowers and fields
in a reason of why it seeks,
what it seeks
until someone spoke to it.
I said: "I loved.
I loved where the young spring of war hit my mundane life
and I heard the man on the radio."
You cannot really stop it when you're falling off of a cliff.
Cloudy greens of fragile hearts,
after death there seems to be nothing to feel.
Only people to awe
by the music of old wheels
pondering from shallow depths to wishes,
fierce stabbing driven by fate.
It wasn't a murder but a bitter-ended dream
that once I felt to belong.

Teenage rage

Nightlit derelict buildings spinning like a rose on silver, that is the beauty of sweat and hunger.

Would you say that the true fruit of life resides so close to its border?

Parted joys of that strange segmentation surely uncalled pleasant – could it be the peak of experience, the peak of human perception, in its blueness and obsession, aesthetically thorough? Ephemeral, unknown titles, saint for unperception and remembered only by uncertain memories that it is, haunting me still. Unexistent love which swam away by runninng youth, a dream of young breath that wants to consume everything physical, harowed either way of receiving or not. During and after, for the lost linger.

Awake theatre
Gems beneath slumbering dust on a sewing machine
on the behalf of catatonic mystery.
It was full.
Symbols of youth
and deadly exhaustion,
awake and threatening by its founds towards wounded poems.
Come pay a visit!
We have a hanging stripper,
if you get lost a seagull will carry you home.
The dolls are tonight playing soldiers
and the soldiers are playing meadowbirds,
and I am playing
the jester.

Carpet beater

I was to beat dusty carpets with a carpet beater until
I unrolled one of them. There was a simple funnel with a large ball
inside. It reminded me of lungs, the ball would glow and change
colors every time I breathed in hence I assumed it was a living
creature, I took a closer look: Attic shoes shine like supernovas, by
the fireplace we sit. Everyone does something else. I write as secret
misdeeds lie with spread legs behind the consciousness. You look at
me with your eyes and I feel like a child bored by May cottages
getting Catcher in the Rye for birthday. It's like some canvas of hope
to be allowed to sink into your soul without a trace.

Too much. Too little. The houses without eyes breathe and
bathe in a tank of beer like wild honey dripping down the ears of
everything that will never happen. The bathroom had a view
downhill. One could easily fall to death. Yet to feel and to deem is
not the same: landscapism is a series of chemical reactions that either
make a living disaster or the best thing ever. I threw the carpet away,
oh, tender, secluded hell.

Summer
The bells toll on the bottom of the pool and mockingbirds ring in the
ears.
Day and night, pines are in a play on mystery and the living seems so
easy
even with the last May when there was nothing left but to watch
a bee so thriving to fertilize
florets near campsite affections.
You were paralyzed. They gave you a mitten blanket, letting you rest
in sleep
for twelve or more hours.
The staggered howling now is distanced in the attic's sky above
a sunburnt treehouse:
tranquility, nothingness.
There has to be found something to express
steel gentle sprinkles of heavy laundry.
Must I sleep
on the sun's surface
in a linen carriage
wheeling through idle loss,
while the lost missing
is the feeling of blueness from loves – one like another.
I seek like everyone else does and everything that has
happened to me was heaven.
As if I wasn't there. The ambulance didn't even look at me.

Revolt of Pisces

to Samo "Sunshine" K.
Cancerous trees above the sky
shimmer
with the oblivion of earth below
and its cities
as angels climb the sugar pots
and nude men swim in liquid thunder.
Always have I felt to be controlled by someone or something.
Parents, system, school
and anyone cruder than sky lake kingdom,
and men that have still seemed brutal, calculating,
as if most of them carried wasps in a paper bag,
trouching with a dislocated knee,
as if I was since birth circled upon in order for me not to become
what I did.
They show us what we want to see and we like what they present
but fear is only the kitsch of old animosity.
Tonight,
2 am at the square.
Bring the Spanish guitar too,
at least for a while.

Memoirs on the party
Remember?
I bestowed you a notebook just a little larger, yet identical to mine.
The one I own
still has blood on it from the sombers of
how your cigar smell and pearly whitened teeth aged into
a somewhery remnant,
not even as thick as a single human hair,
on a foil of my gray stewed brain.
I suppose people are way more likable and smarter when drunk
but for some reason, adults assume connections are made
when both of us play violin or both of us have a cat,
that ashen lady who wanders off too far.
But I insist all that is true in this world must be a divine deal no one
truly understands
nor it needs to be understood,
only experienced, felt through.
Thereby I felt,
unfortunately something less.
I came to surrender to spoilt frivolities old like moldy boots
and as all the philosophers in the living room
arrived uncanny and drunk
by the possessive weedy desire of dreams,
we both agreed on what to do:
"I have to note this treachery of yours down.
That will get me nice royalties."

Unpeace

I. Defined control

Humans apprehend the sorrow of loss by death thereby why do they fail if it comes to the loss of their own will?

Dense blue waters might have been the vale of transcendation that bothers the hollow deputized crowd. Weaved tunics of sand, weaved by pines, capture less prevalent sights. Good morning limbo, loneliness of these waters shall be the peak, just not now. Teenage lunging birds suffering of social or sexual hunger of which graveyard is unknown. Perhaps a sonorous island or the collective consciousness of part-time housewives.

Aloof, addicted to eternity's murder. It's a love greater than unwritten laws: your home has another place. I stand, my name is James Dean. I come of lingered noon. Scraped shitted-on bricks have a tender danger to them. That's what we got for birthday as the cruelest joke of your friend. It could have been a worse celebration if it'd had fringes or a tick in the eye. At least out of those bricks a house can be built while we chant Yogi's song: "You, me and Orwen at the bottom of the lake." We burst out of nylon age, thrown somewhere for none to produce hope on our own. People shouldn't even want to lose their human ego entirely. One who learns to fly no longer wants to walk, at least not like in previous times, in mud and fumes of polished limbless sculptures, eyeing women judging within borders of contributed suburb views on a coil sunflower. Mud, yes, we are scolded to trudge in turd just for living in swamps. Who flies is a monkey, they screech. There should be a want to liberate our belongings, however then it would flee to orange clouds unreturning to the parental nest.

II. Float

Prepare the escape. And prepare it well. Powder atrocities moved by herbaries, buy a lot of fruit, grow out your pubic hair, study aviatics: loneliness has left us here. Use your heart to burn your clothed body until it gets outside making you fly on passion, the force of tender gardens… swans hold their necks proud, a flowing tea urges pulse, airplanes, engines. Must swans be keen on qualmed turn from watery gates.

"Take the bird's weight upon your wings."
Collected paintings of Elliotté P. Joel
(2016-2023)

Hole, 2022
acrylic paint, cardboard

The Horse & The Storm, 2022
acrylic paint

Opium, 2022
acrylic paint, newspaper, plastic, wood
also known as *Elliotté and Erik*

Secret Rooms, 2022
acrylic paint, silk, paper fringes, cardboard

Glass Relations, 2022
acrylic paint, wood

The Forest, 2022
acrylic paint, cardboard

Glass Relations – Friend, 2022
acrylic paint, wood

The Eclipse of Subconscious, 2022
acrylic paint, newspaper, cotton, plastic, cardboard

Title Unknown, 2023
acrylic paint
To Milan

Uphill Garden, 2022
acrylic paint

Ginger, 2022
acrylic paint, paper fringes

Love, 2022
acrylic paint
Joel's submission to Maľba 2022 Award

Summer on Uranus, 2016
acrylic paint
The first part of three cycles

Three Corners, 2022
acrylic paint
To Martin Klimo

Title Unknown, 2023
acrylic paint

Title Unknown, 2022
acrylic paint, cotton, newspaper, polyester
To Joel's mother

Title Unknown, 2022
acrylic paint
To Amália Komorová

Festivities, 2022
acrylic paint, cardboard

Title Uknown, 2019
acrylic paint, wood
The second part of three cycles

"Make love very tenderly."
Poetry of Elliotté P. Joel

Feral artist

to Lukrécia

I want to stay in bed and dream just a little longer.

I want to detangle all the carousels. I want to tell all the people that most of the time they don't know that they know the truth.

But square meter I don't own roars out morning trains with umbrellas under a roof, attacking skulls crave subtle touch. I put a knife on their nude hands: bring me residue of your partle entropy that'll bestow me the warmth of wolves. Cats are out on the streets already.

Who taught me to write? My head. My head comes from its own lies and truths that once were or weren't on a steep white hill without grass, without trees and it felt so lonesome, yet free.

To profoundly come to terms with unity one needs to be alone. Does the world reflect me for I don't happen to be the reflection of world on its own? Thereby do the works of my mind reflect the mind of yours? There is a balding woman full of codeine and a cold-skin snake of seven miles. They are alive, you see. They want to be your friends. And they cannot speak:

In the East they call me
American whore
and in the West they call me
Eastern block pushover.
The childbirth was hurried
within the blackness of rubber aggregate walls and roadless jeweled
sky.
The only missing piece is the light,
a dayless frozen bead of hope I forgot in a stolen blue bus cold
enough for aloud lunatics:
the stones bled and my world was made of liberty.

Manifesto of wild days

Unfar soon disappearance was the result of cradled life and hot streams on these wild days like beautiful butterflies scrambled on feces and by evening on intimidating dark logs. Choppy alienations breastfeed freely on salted screams. Yellow skies overwash dry breaking collars for dogs. I don't want to return home. I don't want to return, asleep street radiate.

The needles will keep sewing the hemp tighter around my ovaries since the second of my return and it's not worth the clean bed. I would rather have Black Mary for breakfast and nothing more.

The soul shall lead me through writing. The soul shall know the books not read are my favorite ones, I choose to live, not within the coldest neon of father's furthest heart, yet within a candle trucing to let my eyes see the sun with a release of taught blindness.

Gone Elliotté
The wind
it was the wind
who took me
to its prism catacombs
inside iridescent hill
reclaiming my body
to nature
and my soul
to its flowing tail.

Unfelt

to Yelyzaveta Shyhida

In order to understand, one has to experience the exact polarity of the given subject. Freezing wooden skelets letter fall leaves dove's flight. Hard sugar has reached sweetness and the drums have been taken, only the silence remnated.

She gets fresh tulips every week, yet the yells she is bestowed every day of human forbidden heartbeat... seeding machines, not people. Leading insensitive tongues sheet their parts in camomile water, dry then inflated, and wet, then sunk. There are no seasons. Cherries fall on her young breasts.

Fern pathways
Pinecone dresses and fern's secret steps
perfume the late-night tea of yesterday's fog
and it appears so insignificant to whoever's seeks
but the wilderness within:
freed, trimmed or cemented nerve extensions of unconsciousness.

Raw breath

to You

If you don't go to sleep you don't have to wake up.
And wait for them to abandon their lovers.
Films of white paint snow on their graves.

Loon

to E. S.

Birds shutter in summer trees. Some people don't trust seatbelts and some people don't trust other people.

Water foam and round breeze eat everything whole. Siren lagoons are on a diet and small javelins downrise whilst immaculate symphony of rain: the lips are plump, dry in heavy breaking skulls. Almost like kissing blooming petals. These holidays are way more suicidal than any other we've seen.

Long dog spoons – fallen spiderweb spice of nature's duties – understand "my love, my muse"... Yet can a profound love be a great muse and can the great muse be profound love? We are like brawling ghosts of city, alone and drunken searching time and space, unable to surmise the objective of our crocodile lookings. Put down all the candles like communards when you'll be bored next time. Behead their wayed waxed strings. Make them not burn and make my heart rest in seizures as vessels wrestle for twenty-one winters and deep crush to moonlight is the noisemaker of looking room. Sapphire-walled pores beat in thwarting peace, liquids are dry and I am clean.

Thereby snows come to seed the happy unawareness of manic runs. Pointing boulevard st. protects nighted souls and their uneven flights of the oldest youth, loon-bitten farths.

Know the rain

To E. S.

Eyes like gentle seaweeds of cotton rain
and lips,
and nose,
are ethereal sand levitating by shaman's music,
could it be the heaven
to ponder,
heaven's mind?
Only if we could sit down
by whistling street and I would teach you
to know the rain
of your hardships,
and you would teach me
to know the wind
of my sorrows,
and learn to walk
in the rain and wind
hand-to-hand.
Erik,
Erik, here we stand,
flawed and yellow
from dandelion doubts,
prepared well
with weapons
and strategy
and healthcare
to fight the undead what has hurt.
My love, we should know the rain
by its treacherous lurid dance.

An oak eye

to E. S.

You touch my hand in the music of glass waves on the rising
lighthouse.
The sight on a glimpse of an oak eye
uncertain,
fragile,
sharp with enigmatic perseverance that could troop
even the highest-embracing grass
like mountains in television on which nothing grows.
You kiss me as if nothing could fall apart.

Facing none

to You

People act conventionally out of fear of punishment, seclusion. Seclusion challenges self. And nobody in fact trusts themself.

I no longer refuse to slumber on meadows. Low needleness possess swallow birds during their unwarned flight, swinging sax of soon-to-be clouded skies. Cartilage prisons of lotus scarlet fever cannot see very well and septuagenarian cabbage does not have eyeballs at all, there are some poems that remain unfinished and some I never started… but who was the one I was making love to last thunder, within a soft choke he twisted and the ceaseless waves made me think of angels of Bohemia, the nightly memorial presence with etherealness sought by those who sought nothing, yet everything.

Gentle and beaten, flowing fire of erotic attacks. Haunted in abandonment like a birdhouse full of wasps. Freedom – liberté, are both presence and disappearance.

Indictable banshees, engulfed, deplorable: Every winter I ask myself, trying to remember how it was like to live in summer.
- burning rooves on linen starvation,
- green stables without horses (They have gone. I wonder where.),
- the freshness of youth seemed to be beating time for the past weeks,
- devils have left the hell and disinfected brains took what they could (The best was what I haven't understood).

Oh, to be caught. Beautiful bluegrass capture again.

I lied

Last time some beans in the shed were blue or even grey because the harvest was dry like a lying bull's blooded nose.

This time the basket with grandma's plum cake and grandson's poems fell into the river. Coming ducks surrounded it and the streams rowed it out too far, to the blurred soft horses with copperhair of drawing sand.

He swore that those wild horses pacing the fireground would decimate every aspect that was tamed by high voices likewise short bare smell of nature brought oxygen to the heart and back, healing all the sores of marzipan and peppermint walls in liminal children's room for one second. Hortensia, he named the river, it was a brave and feminine name in desolate leather shoes, and she had to deal with fish just like fish had to deal with her. And this woman doesn't tell you what to think of life nor how to live it.

Orphan baby blue in round wooden frames, scratched bonnets from cousin's memory: I lied, I lied. I didn't eat, I reveried of strong lions far far away from our home.

Sailors meet again

Up there in Kysuce was a cow who loved to pay respect to Ernest Hemingway because she would come to you alone to the pub and lead you home. When we sold her she walked over 13 kilometers through the mountains to be found in front of the door the next morning. The cow lived in good health until she stood up and walked up to the river that took her.

Wet todays and intact washed-over stones that never felt the absolute brutality of human product sense the waves with their feet, and they say: "Bat's cove tremble, lament for sailor affection by their lonely sleep like the song everyone abhors but dances to it as if wild child. Lament for sailor affection by their lost sleep like meeting own souls that are foreigners to themselves. What a curse of an animal woman! Her ghost will never leave you alone. She will whisper to your rocks and climb your spine during widthless sweater altitudes, gloomed violet death, amethyst death…"

Grandfather's grass
We have sold the fields,
no longer witnessing when the wind comes,
encrypted by the daunted storms and grandfather's grass
finds to be bitten by the moon, yet still shining
in just a slight summerlate coldness.

If I was to be eternal,
progressively losing all of my memory on mundane days
and voices,
and names I had loved,
would I keep the nature only,
within the essence it recalls in my body:
living ultimately among life itself,
possessing a sould among a bigger one.

We have sold the fields in such a
ponderous weather – soon to rain –
as if the deity cried along with I.

August flied away like a brief fume of present.

Saloon legs
We brought the mattress
to an uphill field,
the clocks were buried
with all its pale colors.
Throw it to the dogs!
Why would we desire time in a place like this?

Dashed
jump on the featherbed
in bendable dreams of reality.
To live is to sleep very deeply.
Your saloon legs are of feathers, too.
Just to pass the quill to another
so they can
walk barefoot
and cry
with eyes wide open.

1 hour

1 hour of tremor. 1 hour of restless dancing shoes unsuitably borrowed for a funeral by godmother's friend. (Her biscuits have very little butter and crumble in between fingertips.)

Mountainous pans are labile enough to carry the music playing here. (Music speaks. It will tell your pros and vices.)

I suppose few people have seen an angel who had fallen on the dirty floor of Earth for one second and never recovered from it even when he's returned to heaven.

He is still afraid to blink. It's already been one hour.

Susana

You are dry from screams, morrow mourn's abditory, as winterfog clenches, dwelling in your dream of unperceived life. All we truly have is our present time lulled by wild garlic growing from a broken postbox, unpainted and eaten by rust, assessed by red ants in its underrooves. Pilgrimage is to strive beneath that time, Susana, yet all you worship is you of fever, you of sleep, unreturning still in distance further above fields.

They want to look for you despite echoes: you, unfound. Bound by the starlets of snow that stain the lips pink.

Sex

Veiny wrists, veiny faces, through the scare of loneliness goes the screaming snow of change, as clean, as bloody, as wild cherries beneath a lucky girl's curtain. There is some luck in some life in fulfillment of needs as soon as they arise with a steaming hook caught on someone else's rib. Station to station, size zero brunettes and sparked teenage boys deepen old doctor's coffin with the sorrow of how he used to seek a soul too similar, knock door to door and broken elevators made him piss himself and weep, and then he became frowned of adulthood. It's too late for surgical removal: the organs around learned to accede the burning hook's everlasting presence. Rendered flames on open water and the ducks I've killed of fooled wrath laughed the teethiest way, veiny phalluses, through the human scare of loneliness.

Ghetto fame

to anonymous literary critic

That damned book only has two reviews. The first one says that it's wasted money and something so depressing shouldn't have ever been published. The second review was good, but not too good, it was written by me (I didn't know it will show my name).

Another time I borrowed that thing from library and the last pages had many drops of blood. Somebody bled on the book.

I heard at least ten positive commentaries, yet only verbal. I wonder why people talk so much about hate and so little about love. So little that they expect me having created an entire book burdensome, with a wrathful desire to bring others despair, the stew to poison their tongues, burn their intestines and dissolve their bladders.

Yet, do the deathbirds, the ugly ones, scream for humans? Their chilling caws sound not foreign to different feathers, by words they speak, speak of own nature just as they breathe and fly. Me, I write in order to write. I am aware that it cooks your bones exactly like you are aware of the fact that you no longer know how to caw.

The rook was made of a paper catalog found on the ground and one right hand with five fine nails that all had a look of hunger. Turtles and birds, speak! Tell them! Elevate the dust of belonging though it doesn't belong. There are no wrinkles in time because we laminated it with books and albums, cans greased by the black, neglected. Burning sage is like turning on the record and the words are deaf recognition of the all-soul blues stirred but by those who do not understand it.

My anger from upbringing could set plains of saffrons on fire.

The forced dishes of decomposing corpses were never so high above, never so scoffing. I have decided that once I live alone I shall only eat five meals: vegetables, fruits, tea and beer, and potatoes on occasion. It was a foolish thought to humans. Like every thought. What is not foolish to them is but stuff they need not to think about. Trapped lies boiling their lemons on horse's watery eyelids, blunt pain is worse, pop plastic bags below my head only to assure I will not get anywhere with these dreams of philosophy, poetry and peace. Nonetheless, I don't sense being alive less than any regular cleaning lady or any regular mortgage assistant, only in a different way. There is no duty to be special but a duty to identify and express the true root of my flawed perceiving, which thereby led to the discovery that I indeed am not alone and I indeed am a piece of many, nude, imperfect, comprehending.

They say it's the hardest test to indeed pursue oneself against family likewise we may interpret the catalog as the rook – caged and bordered feminity. The rook had a little heart, the heart had a hole so I fucked it. The stale hell of North has begun to melt the day he ate my heart. Bestowed upon the strawberry moon I have won even without the tusks. I adore the unity we feel from left-behind misery so the joy of those who had abandoned the hardships may finally breathe.

In a gleaming gallop, where your touch blackens the paper, where the train pulls you through tunnels and forests in which you see yourself burn as you both sled an acute autumn hill, there the path is formed by walking. Not even the eye of an ostrich can surmise why writing exposes the evil within you. Thus your spirit remains clean. Thus the book remains vile. Let me be. Just close the book or burn it.

Track kisses

to J.

Scent of cigarette smoke along with scent of something else I don't love even a bit. Your mute spiderwebs are circling and they are pale, the eeriness of dark is whelming curtains on the woodern pole and the snakes are growing out of holes like sunbeams. The darkness is whiteness and the light is dark, and it stinks, You stink like all my men I have killed.

But I know, you are the same, of my race: acidulated milk will never stain the rubber of your grey buttons just like wild youth never pegs out in factories, smothered, anaesthetized – I've said that thousand times and I'll say it again – for eternal youth must you be never young.

I want to be with you and feel not. Be without reminiscence and without thoughts, be but once in a while that is dripping. It is the first time that a house breathes with something that is not artificial.

I love my pistol

It was yesterday when Frnka J. died.

Another dead poet I shall forget as I age whereas the world never even got a chance to remember him.

It really isn't about the words people say. Nothing is about muses, intelligence, talent, speed or about how well you fight. It's about the vigilance to survive everything.

To die I'd seen some great poets, three times greater than alcoholic Joel – people who are born once a century. Many of them have overmethed, even more of them have overdrank but most of them have died from day to day without even realizing it. Life has fleed through them and they grew adult (to grow adult is the crudest invention of modern society.)

At least I had the dignified luck to experience their soul, stand next to it and learn so that after the poet passed I could treacherously steal what I can.

A stranger in the flowerbed

Do not believe me, lilies. Not a single word. I do not love you, I just want to make distilled liquor. The dryness on living oil from the fat of my deathmask, sister.

You have caressed all the Western suns. You have kissed all the Western suns and I poetry only. You mustn't believe me, lilies, I lie and I am haggard from twenty-kilometer walks, and starving. Lillies, Amelies, you have slept over the whole Wien. I have nowhere to live. I was raised by places and people that do not exist. I do not come from here. Do not believe me, lilies, not even a word. And shut up. Sleep. I will be lying next to you, listening to the screams of doves in our sheets.

I want to overdose but I am too lazy. Kill me, lilies. Amelies are spreading across the bushiest flowerbeds and grasping them like everything they swallow. Do not believe me, lilies. I am a fool and a killer.

Long days on falcon ridge

to Milan

Rattlesnakes upon butcher's eye. I wanted to look revolting, it was my way to speak. I hated being inside, I just could not sit still and suddenly I had to bake my ass on a chair for eight hours at school. I couldn't lunge or run around so I walked. I didn't talk to anyone and I always had to do something, I shook my legs, picked my skin, scratched paint from everything, pulled my hair. I couldn't stop dreaming of feminine screams of wild meadows. I was young, I was so very young and I knew much more than I do now. "You gentle cow." said a clothed white skeleton with a wig, smoking. I didn't look like a woman nor a man and I was feral and cold, and timid, like a forgotten to-some visionary in bare remembrance, like a toddler who removed their shoes because the feet felt foreign and surgically fake… Yet it's quite timesome now to contemplate fashion or sanity when we could be not contemplating at all. Life is so much better when you're not addicted to anything, addicted to concepts of art, or better, concepts of life. Listen to their arms break – understand everything. Even murder, even people who have children just because they're bored with their existence. And to still love humans and wanting to comprehend them one has to be partly a kind of sociopath. So, the fashion, my fashion in those times was like two boil-blooded birds screeching on a dry mouth, caged larvae expecting disaster in a form of watered red stars. Moss robes air less and less poetry for uncannier reasons. Immense energy is flown here, they don't want to see you, they want to see scandalous perceptions, something that is actually living, like an animal in a zoo slashed and portioned. We might want to love and we still hate.

Pinecones pale green fall too soon

Streams of deserved trains are alive, the drains flow. Birds on electric transmission lines become playful knots by wind. Deaf gypsy is selling vegetables. I am drinking alkaline water on balcony one day before the new semester. I know I am pretty and nobody is really listening to me.

Plucked by raven todays are experienced cars, ride and ride, until there is some essence, rabbits in dreams under a bush, until we are children, and weakened blood pumps in hearts with wild felicity, and even with this I am horrified to death in meadowbees pink-beaded playgrounds.

Hand-held heads to the ground behold sinuses bent over the coldness of tender golden screams, river crushing itself against unkempt green hips, thicker lowland ferns. They pulled me out of the dark service, ripped away from silence where is now no place to close myself behind tears.

Aware, oh aware feathers, death is eating animal's sight in passionate chewing, prolonged onions of grandma's hands pacing slowly in forgotten kindred smiles to last another crude winter, keeping each other warm by sneezing in each other's anuses.

I came here to haunt you by night, whisper poems by duvets, ices touching, erotically rubbing slits, I am the bleeding body of dry grass, dogs wet sniffing tempting to find something alive baptized by hope.

Hair in death of odd numbers, hear a penciled smell of chopped wood and warm illusory closeness of humans. Humans love to die. Nobody wants to live anymore. Just we, magicians can take any form and manifest through the poetry of forbidden expectancy. Eternity prevails even after depriving or loss of physical form. I am pretty with my nature, my dyed ginger, and I'd still be fuckable if I was bald.

A poem to vomit to

What stepfather told me was that in army school (I don't understand why would someone go there from their own mind), in freshman year, his classmate got on the top of the school and tossed himself on an electric fence, dead instantly. He did it because the soldier attire has grown him pimples and the girl who had eyes like fresh olives and a red birthmark exactly between her breasts like an ant carrying its egg, has spitted on the poem he had written to her. "Man needs to be tough. Those who are not will eventually die or end up insane," stepdad said.

That is when I came to analyze what kind of a man am I. I don't think I am a tough man, I am something in between, I am a screamer, but a soul.

I came to the conclusion that perhaps I would have more luck with people if I was given a more common name, like Emma or Lucy, or Veronica. But I cannot bring anyone to talk about this observation. Most of the people really ask me dumb questions. Like who am I. If I was to ask myself who am I, I'd say I am the world. And if you were to ask me who am I, I'd say I am a crude person with a kind heart and a smart person with a quite stupid mind. People are only like what you perceive them to be. I can't really tell you what to deem because you'll do your own anyway.

The woman would scratch herself even a bit with skin ripped open to the meat of her flesh and a dozen of tiny maggots. The pests invaded her tearing-off body the same way I sensed being invaded by the distance of ocean. I have no idea if she died or will have died by the time we find a left-behind forest suitcase and shit inside, closing it forever. In the peripheral tension of death are those scattered stairs made of matte memory, like the dog who brought six strangled hares to his man's doorstep.

Scratch, scratch, grieving sister, observe the car batteries, nuns or lawyers – we are nothing but pigs in an unnamed poem. Yet forecounting all these disgusting things we fail to react unless it's somehow involved with us and our thoughts. To comprehend the nature of humans must you perceive animals first… but now quiet!

The old man is eating, it's time for poison. That might make us some money.

Did I dream?

Was I an alkaline sitting through choir as the ground shook, and shook, until the humans lost their hearts, having them replaced with knives?

The crooks lane
I can see,
I can truly see
the watery blue night
within a yellow flicker
of something wild
and untamed.
"I need some tragedy in my life, really quick!"
I shouted at the switchman along nightly dirts.
In wrath I would wish Him a truly harrowing death
yet I am aware that in case He really ceased
I would bestow fresh flowers on His grave every Sunday.

Like a white powder ballerina
a lamb perched near that sunless house in front of the station
departing from the sunrays cycling down the leaves of trees.
The lamb was idle in a daze for it knew it would be hit very soon
therefore it dreamt of while clouds and one single morning
when it woke up
with a reeling taste of safety.
Birches romped distinguishly, unskilledly in a semi-pitiable way.
The wind broke off through the window rails.
And you always held me as if it was for the first and last time.

Each welcome overstays,
a golden coin ascends through
crooked shameful horns only left to be a mere skeleton.

Mileva Marić

I. Trial
Usage of literature
as an instrument of death.
I tried to defend myself,
I really did.
"What are we, nazis, to burn books?"
You lie down
and I lie near
lightly touching rainy flowers.
Farewell,
the renegades and whilers didn't listen
nor cared to listen.

II. Death sentence
Has she ever gone
with the pain?
A tiger and a bear
feast upon my blood and flesh.
There I become,
there, with joyous hands
and rays of smoke,
withheld
and groundless.
Grey bitches have pebbles in between their teeth
until finally she exclaims:
"First cut her robe
then the breasts!"

III. Hypothesis
It is to purify the chewed up findfull becomes
condemned by the ego
that fears its death more than the death of the soul it represents

for a seventy-something years long trip
of whatever it wishes to achieve,
yet still the majority chooses
materialism and production of offspring
as miserable as they are, if not more.
I shouted:
"Tie my tongue with a rope of poisoned cheese
if my core ever fates to bad roads."
and the guillotine dropped down.

Awoken in a dream

Our parents had to wait in lines to get flour and meat. And we couldn't sense that crudeness of sun nor the wild screams of life. The cleaningness of our mother, furthering touches, Eden, wind. Awoken in a dream, crying. The animosity of world at schools and works, masks on the streets, nature knows no hatred even with all her infiltrations, all for the money, money and fear.

All we could was to hold among the family and our own beliefs in coincidence, and own hopes that we are not insane, yet. Awoken in a dream, crying? No! Only awoken. Awoken with feet on dry ground and under brushy sun on grass next to your abdomen and curls.

You lived in a ghetto near a factory and it stank like something dying, dust and tobacco of your four pipes, herbal tea of the far East. Sakuras, old molds living forever. We are still but learning to live although too soon we'd to discover that no dreams are ever to be forgiven. On dinner we had raw cabbage and one hour of piano.

They'd never caught us with your umbrella above my head and they'd never asked for permission cards of free movement, you were carrying luck within yourself, it seems. You will haunt me for the rest of my life. Even after nightly hours, even in liminal spaces, even whilst speeches of literature, philosophy and loss of yourself for something that has nourished us and suddenly we were pierced by it, and it still hurts

and listeners are still clapping in arousal.

Questions asked

When I die will I be made into a fur coat similar to the one I am wearing? Pressed cartridge in armed summer of balcony speaks? Slow entrances of resentful goose unders brewed by fat and sudden coldness of feet?

When I die will you wait for me to get the beer?

Do all whores rule the nation with an angered iron stove? Is food made of time and is time made of life? And again, the beer? The coat? I don't need to calm down, I need you to listen to me: Why did you fly so high on that plane, was it because your mother's beast rouging along thorns of tongues or was it because you forgot my name sunk, rasberrious beneath? Why did the goat collapse so theatrically at my poor attempts? And can the sky beer resurrect her alive?

Then I fell asleep. On the next mornings I don't tend to remember what I've written, I just saw the holed walls of belonging four pretend that people like me and you go to heaven because we'd sacrificed our torments of loneliness to art. They pretend it very well.

Please, wait for the last poem

Please, wait for the last poem. I cannot promise you it will be
long. And I cannot promise you it will be short. I also cannot
promise you it will be good. But I promise to recite it to you. Wait
just a little longer, please. I want to tell you something different first.

I thought at first that I mustn't be human. I perceived my
moves and facial expressions to be almost robotic, self-taught.
I perceived my face to be very uncanny. Although I have had a few
soul-piercing things happen to me, I can clearly recall feeling
traumatized since I remember. By everything. The intersection of
railways blessed by a thief. Deranged blemishes blessed by its
harrows of teeth. Livers, plainly freezing. If I am a human after all
then I ought to be a profoundly insane one.

As I suppose, after a certain time we disconnect from what
happened. Perhaps then we care about it the same way we care about
dead tales of the past, like wars or crises, or twisted societal notions
– there are people who would scrutinize the occurrences for
entertainment and there are people who cannot even think about the
topic because they find it too horrible. Yet in general we know quite
a lot about suffering and death, and we wonder why did it have to
happen, however, deep down we don't care since it does not affect us
at all and it has nothing to do with our lives because we never had to
experience it.

Yet there is still one thing troubling my sleep that for my
alcohol season I cannot recall very well. (Alcohol did not help.
Instead of memories I dream in feelings I used to feel and smell of
your gentle warm soul.) I smelt your living skin yesterday in the
wind while walking next to a rusty fence on an unkept paddock. I
took a few steps back to look at the fence, yet the fume was as gone
as it has appeared.

Alekai has purchased two boxed wines and we have drank
them before the concert. Mannequins of distressed world, I saw you
between crowds of unaware people. I approached you with a story of
my misery, dancing. Then we made love and the next day we talked

and talked, and made love again. You walked me home for almost 3 miles in the dark. The next day we talked and couldn't stop. I took you to a tea shop on a bicycle, in the night we went to the park, climbing children's slides. You were less sad with me, you said. I met your best friend and you met mine. We got drunk with your cousin and ran across the highway, we went to see a bad movie pretending it was good and I took you to an abandoned house so you can write in peace (you wanted to write a book about a man of lost existence). You took me to your home and played guitar for me very shyly, lying in a cold bed, you gave me your jacket. You used to call me "my wife". Then we went to the market and rode a rollercoaster. That was the last day before they took you. I sent you letters and chocolates, a notebook and a small collage of our few pictures. I waited. I waited very long. I knew you couldn't reply. Yet even after your return you didn't write back.

That's all. Here is the poem that I promised:

Dry branches scream
against the window's glass.
But how?
We have cut down all the trees.

www.ingramcontent.com/pod-product-compliance
Lightning Source LLC
LaVergne TN
LVHW010458200726
843506LV00002B/143